Rob Shu

Eva

G000143794

7.

COOKING
WITH
ENA

ENA THOMAS

Photography:
JOHN EVANS, QUASAR

Illustrations:
RHIAN NEST JAMES

HUGHES

First printed: November 1996

ISBN 0 85284 206 6

Co-ordinated by: Luned Whelan

Typeset and printed in Wales by
Dinefwr Press, Rawlings Road,
Llandybïe, Carmarthenshire.

Published by Hughes a'i Fab,
Parc Tŷ Glas, Llanisien, Caerdydd CF4 5DU.

CONTENTS

5

FOREWORD/RHAGAIR

The publication of this volume of recipes by Ena Thomas, the popular cook on S4C's magazine programme *Heno*, is based on the phenomenal success of the two Welsh books published to date. Combined sales of *Llyfr Ryseitiau Ena* and *Mwy o Ryseitiau Ena* climbed to over 8000 copies in 10 months. This book is for Ena's faithful fans, non-Welsh speakers and learners alike, who will find a useful glossary of Welsh food terms after the main body of recipes. Thanks are due to all the staff at *Heno* and to Ena's fans everywhere, new and old, young and old!

Ena Thomas was born and bred in Felindre, near Swansea, and studied Hotel and Catering Management and Training in London at 17 years of age. On completing her course, Ena worked in the private wing of the Catering Department at the University of London College Hospital. She was also trained by Mr. P. H. Venning, who became a catering officer at Buckingham Palace. Ena taught catering to adults in various centres for the former Dyfed Education Authority for 30 years. She lives in Carmarthen with her husband Geoff, and enjoys spending time with her two sons and five grandchildren.

Croeso i argraffiad newydd sbon o ryseitiau Ena Thomas. Yn wahanol i'r cyfrolau a gyhoeddwyd eisoes, mae'r llyfr hwn yn Saesneg, i alluogi Cymry di-Gymraeg a dysgwyr i gael blas ar ryseitiau cogyddes boblogaidd y gyfres *Heno* ar S4C. Oherwydd llwyddiant ysgubol *Llyfr Ryseitiau Ena* a *Mwy o Ryseitiau Ena*, penderfynwyd cyflenwi'r galw am ehangu'r gynulleidfa all greu campweithiau yn y gegin beth bynnag yw iaith yr aelwyd. Rhaid diolch i bawb sy'n gweithio yn *Heno* a 'ffans' Ena, yn hen a newydd, ym mhob man.

STARTERS

TOMATO, CUCUMBER AND CAERPHILLY CHEESE SALAD

Ingredients
The Salad
450g/1 lb large tomatoes
1 large cucumber
450g/1 lb Caerphilly cheese
1 loaf French bread

The Dressing
6 tbs olive oil
3 tbs wine vinegar
1 clove garlic, crushed
1 tbs chopped parsley

Method
- Slice the tomatoes and cucumber thinly.

- Slice the cheese, and arrange alternate slices of tomato, cucumber and cheese on a serving plate.

- Mix all the ingredients of the dressing thoroughly.

- Pour the dressing over the tomato, cucumber and cheese.

- Serve with warm French bread.

> **TIP: This salad is ideal as a tasty supper on a summer evening.**

CARMARTHEN HAM WITH FRUIT MEDLEY

A lovely brunch for summer, easy to make and delicious to eat.

Ingredients
1 small Galia melon
4 passion fruit
115g/4 oz seedless grapes
115g/4 oz Carmarthen ham, thinly sliced
freshly ground black pepper to taste
115g/4 oz fresh or frozen raspberries
parsley to garnish

Method
- Cut the melon in half, and de-seed. Cut into thin slices.

- Cut the passion fruit into quarters.

- Place the folded slices of ham along one side of a large serving plate.

- Arrange the fruit on the plate around the ham – be as artistic as you like!

- Season the ham with the black pepper.

- Garnish with the parsley.

MELON IN GINGER SAUCE

This was originally part of a Mother's Day menu. It is simple to make, tasty and colourful.

Ingredients
1 Galia melon
1 Cantaloupe melon
225g/8 oz plain yoghurt
5 tsp ginger syrup
2 pieces preserved stem ginger, finely chopped
pinch nutmeg
chives to garnish

Method
- Halve the melons, then remove seeds using a teaspoon or melon baller.

- Scoop the melon into ball shapes and place them in a serving dish.

- Mix together the yoghurt, chopped ginger, syrup and nutmeg.

- Pour over the melon and garnish with the chives.

> **TIP: You can prepare this in individual serving dishes or one large dish – it is very pretty in glass dishes.**

HARVEST SOUP

Ingredients
25g/1 oz butter
450g/1 lb carrots, peeled and cubed
1 onion, peeled and sliced
2 potatoes, peeled and cubed
1 red pepper and 1 green pepper, de-seeded and finely chopped
50g/2 oz lentils
salt and pepper
1 bay leaf
40g/ an ounce and a half plain flour
150ml/ a quarter pint of water
450 ml/ three quarters of a pint of stock
115g/4 oz grated Cheddar cheese
parsley to garnish

Method
- Melt the butter and fry all the vegetables until soft.

- Add the stock, lentils, the salt and pepper and simmer for 30 minutes.

- Mix the flour with the water and add to the soup. Stir well until the soup thickens.

- Add the cheese and parsley to the soup, stirring until the cheese has melted. Pour into tureen.

- Serve with *croutons* or Bacon and Herb Bread (see p. 93)

SALMON MOUSSE

Ingredients
1 400g/14 oz tin of red salmon
175g/6 oz mayonnaise
175g/6 oz *fromage frais*
2 tbs brandy
salt and pepper
175g/6 oz *crème fraîche*
pinch cayenne pepper
a few drops Tabasco sauce
lemon juice

Method
● Drain the salmon and place in a food processor with all the other ingredients.

● Blend until the mixture is smooth.

● Adjust seasoning to taste.

● Serve in individual ramekin dishes.

● Serve with Melba toast, lettuce and tomato.

> **TIP: *This freezes well for Christmas.***
> ***Remove from the freezer two hours before serving.***

MUSHROOM ROAST PEPPERS

Ingredients

2 large red peppers
450g/1 lb fresh tomatoes
2-3 crushed garlic cloves
1 onion, finely chopped
2 tbs olive oil
25g/1 oz Muscavado sugar
salt and pepper

1 tbs tomato *purée*
50g/2 oz mushrooms
50g/2 oz flaked almonds
1 tbs mint, finely chopped
50g/2 oz bacon, cooked and chopped
50g/2 oz Parmesan cheese

Method

- Cut the peppers in half lengthways and remove the core and seeds. Place on a baking tray.

- Plunge the tomatoes in boiling water for 2-3 minutes, peel and halve, removing the seeds. Chop finely.

- Chop the mushrooms and fry quickly in hot fat with the onion, garlic and bacon and stir well. Add the finely chopped tomatoes and the *purée* and stir again. Add the almonds, sugar and mint to the mixture.

- Fill the peppers with the mixture. Cook in the oven for 15 minutes at 200C/400F/Gas 6.

- Serve with a lettuce garnish.

TIP: This is a very tasty dish for vegetarians if you substitute the bacon with 50g/2 oz nuts of your choice, finely chopped __not__ ground.

VEGETABLE SOUP WITH CHEESY BREAD

What could be better on a cold day than good hot soup, with tasty cheesy bread?

Ingredients
The Soup
1 leek, sliced
1 onion, sliced
1 carrot, cubed
1 stick celery, finely chopped
1 red pepper
115g/4 oz cabbage, cut in strips
1 400g/14 oz tin tomatoes, chopped
1 tbs white wine vinegar
1 tbs Demerara sugar
400g/14 oz butter beans
a few drops chilli sauce
1 tbs olive oil
2 cloves garlic, crushed
750ml/ a pint and a half of vegetable stock
2 tbs finely chopped herbs (basil, coriander, parsley)

The Bread
1 slice bread without crust for each person (cut in circles to fit individual soup dishes)
50g/2 oz butter
1 clove garlic, crushed
25g/1 oz Parmesan cheese for each person

Method
- Prepare the vegetables as above.

- Heat the oil in a large pan and fry the onion, leek, carrot and celery for 5 minutes.

- Add the tomatoes, garlic, vinegar, sugar, chilli sauce and stock. Bring to the boil and simmer for 15 minutes.

- Add the cabbage and butter beans and cook for a further 5 minutes until the soup is lovely and thick. Add salt and pepper to taste.

- To prepare the bread, first melt the butter and mix in the garlic.

- Spread the garlic butter over the bread and sprinkle the cheese on top. Bake the circles in the oven for 10 minutes at 200C/400F/Gas 6.

- Place a circle of bread on top of each bowl of soup and sprinkle with the fresh herbs.

STUFFED TOMATOES

A delicious summer savoury, ideal as a starter or a light lunch – and healthy!

Ingredients

4 large tomatoes
3 spring onions, chopped
2 pineapple rings, chopped
115g/4 oz Carmarthen ham, or
    cooked chicken or turkey
1 tbs fresh basil, finely chopped
1 clove garlic, crushed
salt and pepper

1 tbs tomato *purée*
225g/8 oz *couscous*
275 ml/ half a pint of pineapple
    juice
4 slices bread
25g/1 oz butter
1 tsp mixed herbs
50g/2 oz Parmesan cheese, grated

Method

- Cut the tops off the tomatoes, remove seeds and cores. Place in an ovenproof dish.

- Boil the pineapple juice and pour over *couscous* in a bowl. Cover and leave for 10 minutes until the *couscous* has absorbed all the juice and become fluffy.

- To the *couscous*, add the ham, spring onions, pineapple, tomato *purée*, garlic and basil.

- Fill the tomatoes with the *couscous*, sprinkle with Parmesan cheese and place in the oven for 10 minutes at 200C/400F/ Gas 6.

- To make the *croutons*, brush the slices of bread with the melted butter and sprinkle with mixed herbs before placing under the grill or in a non-stick frying pan until golden brown.

- Serve each tomato on one *crouton*, pour some tomato juice around them and garnish with watercress.

LEEK AND MUSHROOM SALAD

Ingredients
450g/1 lb baby leeks
2 tbs olive oil
225g/8 oz mushrooms
6 tbs white wine
1 tbs parsley, finely chopped
1 tbs chives
1 clove garlic, crushed
115g/4 oz smoked salmon
salt and pepper

Method

- Heat the oil in a large pan, add the mushrooms and garlic and cook for 5 minutes.

- Add the wine and leeks and cook until the wine is reduced.

- Remove from the heat and stir in the parsley and chives. Add salt and pepper to taste.

- Arrange on a small serving plate and scatter strips of smoked salmon over the top.

- Serve with warm French bread.

TIP: If you don't eat fish, chop Teifi cheese (or whichever is your favourite cheese) over the salad.

LEEK AND POTATO SOUP

Ingredients
2 large leeks
1 onion
50g/2 oz butter
450g/1 lb potatoes
570ml/1 pint chicken stock
salt and pepper
225ml/8 fl oz fresh double cream
chives or watercress to garnish
1 loaf French bread

Method
- Clean all the vegetables and chop finely.

- Melt the butter in a large pan and gently fry the onion for 1 minute.

- Add the leeks, potatoes, stock, salt and pepper. Bring to the boil and simmer for 20 minutes.

- Purée the soup in a blender or through a sieve.

- Just before serving, add the cream and re-heat (*without* boiling).

- Garnish with chives, and serve with chunks of French bread.

FISH

PAN FRIED TOWY SEWIN

Ingredients
4 175g/6 oz sewin fillets
1 bunch spring onions
2 tbs olive oil
1 tbs butter
salt and pepper
275ml/half a pint of dry white wine
juice of 1 lemon
50g/2 oz smoked bacon

Method
- Remove any bones from the fillets.

- Season and sprinkle with lemon juice.

- Heat the oil and butter in a pan, add the sewin and fry gently for 1 minute each side.

- Add the bacon, spring onions and wine, bring to the boil and cook for 1 minute.

- Serve on a bed of crisp vegetables and fried potatoes.

OYSTERS WITH RED PEPPER SAUCE

Oysters are in season from September to April. They're best served chilled and raw, as a first course with lemon and Tabasco sauce.

Ingredients
20 oysters
1 red pepper
150ml/ a quarter pint of olive oil
2 tsp grated fresh ginger
1 tbs dill, finely chopped
2 tsp soured cream

Method

- Clean the beards off the oysters.

- Open each one, keeping the liquor, and remove the oysters from the shells.

- Clean the shells thoroughly and place on a serving plate.

- Poach the oysters in their own liquor for 3 minutes and put to one side.

- Halve the pepper and de-seed, then grill with the skin side up until the skin splits.

- Peel the skin off and chop pepper finely.

- Blend the pepper, olive oil, liquor, ginger, dill and soured cream in a food processor until smooth.

- Replace the oysters in their shells and pour the sauce over them, then garnish with lemon, strips of pepper and dill.

TIP: Use the same sauce with Salmon and Trout Mousse on page 32.

TROUT WITH HERB AND NUT STUFFING

Ingredients
4 trout
50g/2 oz butter
1 tblsp olive oil
salt and pepper
150ml/ a quarter pint of white wine
4 shallots, sliced
1 tblsp parsley
1 tblsp basil
115g/4 oz white breadcrumbs
115g/4 oz hazelnuts
1 tblsp chives
2 lemons

Method

- Wash and clean the trout, leaving the heads and tails on but removing the bones.

- Heat the oil and butter in a large pan, place the trout in it and cook gently for 5 minutes each side.

- Pour in the wine and simmer for a further 5 minutes. Place the fish on a plate and keep warm.

- Add the shallots, nuts, breadcrumbs and herbs to the pan. Cook until golden and scatter over the trout.

- Garnish with the lemons and serve with new potatoes, broccoli and carrots.

FISH CAKES

This recipe is great for using up leftover potato with a tin of salmon for a lovely light lunch or super supper.

Ingredients
450g/1 lb mashed potatoes
400g/14 oz red salmon
2 tbs parsley, finely chopped
1 tsp mustard
1 egg
rind of 1 lemon
115g/4 oz white breadcrumbs
275ml/half a pint of natural yoghurt
juice of 1 lemon
50g capers, finely chopped

To Fry
a little flour
2 eggs

Method

- Place the mashed potato in a large bowl. Drain the salmon, removing any black skin.

- Add the salmon to the potato, parsley, lemon rind, mustard, egg and breadcrumbs. Mix thoroughly.

- Turn the mixture out onto a floured board and form into a long sausage shape. Cut into 12 equal portions, and shape into rounds half an inch (1.5cm) thick.

- Beat the two eggs and dip each cake in the liquid. Then cover in breadcrumbs and fry for about 3 minutes each side.

- Mix the yoghurt, lemon juice and capers well.

- Serve the fish cakes and sauce with salad and new potatoes.

TIP: Leave the fish cakes in the fridge for a while before dipping in egg and breadcrumbs – they're much easier to handle when cooled through.

TUNA CRUMBLE

Ingredients
Tuna Mix
50g/2 oz butter
275ml/half a pint of milk
1 red pepper and 1 green pepper, finely chopped
bunch of spring onions
175g/6 oz broccoli florets
50g/2 oz plain flour
150ml/ a quarter pint of white wine
115g/4 oz button mushrooms
1 400g/14 oz tin tuna in brine
salt and pepper

The Crumble
175g/6 oz fresh white breadcrumbs
50g/2 oz wholemeal flour
3 tbs Parmesan cheese
50g/2 oz hazelnuts, finely chopped

Method
- Gently fry the vegetables in a little olive oil and butter for 2-3 minutes.

- Pour the milk, wine, butter and flour into a saucepan and whisk well over a medium heat until the sauce thickens. Season with salt and pepper.

- Add the vegetables, tuna and basil to the sauce. Transfer to an ovenproof dish.

- Mix the ingredients of the crumble together thoroughly and spread over the tuna mix. Bake for 20 minutes at 200C/ 400F/ Gas 6.

SALMON IN CHEESE SAUCE

This is a simple recipe for a lovely supper. It's useful if guests are coming, since it's easy to prepare beforehand.

Ingredients
The Salmon
4 salmon fillets
salt and pepper
juice of 1 lemon

The Sauce
50g/2 oz butter
50g/2 oz plain flour
570ml/1 pint of milk
115g/4 oz mature Cheddar cheese, grated
chives, finely chopped

Method

- Place the salmon fillets in an ovenproof dish, and sprinkle the lemon juice and salt and pepper over them.

- To make the sauce: place the milk, butter and flour in a saucepan and whisk over the heat until the sauce is thick and glossy. Stir in the cheese until it melts.

- Add salt and pepper and chives, and pour the sauce over the salmon.

- Pipe mashed potato around the edge of the dish.

- Cook in the oven for 15 minutes at 200C/400F/Gas 6.

- Serve with baby carrots.

COCKLE, POTATO AND LEEK PIE IN A WINE SAUCE

Ingredients

The Cockles

225g/8 oz cockles
450g/1 lb leeks, finely chopped
225g/8 oz potatoes, chopped
570ml/1 pint of white wine
50g/2 oz butter
50g/2 oz plain flour
salt and pepper
275ml/half a pint of single cream

The Piecrust

225g/8 oz plain flour
115g/4 oz butter
half a teaspoon salt
2 tbs parsley
3-4 tbs water
1 egg

Method

- Place the cockles, leeks and potatoes in a saucepan with the wine.

- Bring to the boil and cook for 15 minutes.

- Bind together the butter and flour and add to the mixture; bring back to the boil and cook for a further 2-3 minutes. Add the cream.

- Pour into a pie dish and leave to cool.

- Prepare the piecrust, first rubbing the butter into the flour. Add the salt and parsley, gradually adding the water to make a soft, firm dough (you may not need all the water).

- Roll the dough out to the same size as the piedish and place over the mixture.

- Brush with egg and bake for 15 minutes at 200C/400F/Gas 6.

SALMON AND TROUT *MOUSSE*

Ingredients
225g/8 oz smoked salmon
2 large trout
50g/2 oz cooked prawns
225g/8 oz low fat soft cheese
2 tbs chives, finely chopped
2 tbs lemon juice
2-3 drops Tabasco sauce
packet of gelatine

The Sauce
2 red peppers
4 tomatoes
2 garlic cloves, crushed
1 tblsp tomato *purée*
3 tbs pesto sauce

Method

- Line 4 ramekin dishes with smoked salmon, letting the salmon overlap the sides.

- Cover the trout in clingfilm and cook in the microwave for 10 minutes. Remove the skin, then take the fish from the bones.

- Whizz the trout, soft cheese, lemon juice and Tabasco sauce in a blender for 1 minute.

- Add the prawns and chives. Melt the gelatine in 3 tablespoons of boiling water and pour in to the mixture.

- Divide the mixture between the ramekin dishes and cover with the overlapping salmon. Refrigerate for an hour before serving with the sauce, new potatoes and seasonal vegetables.

- To make the sauce: de-seed the peppers and tomatoes and roughly chop, then place in a saucepan with the garlic, tomato *purée*, 6 tablespoons of water and plenty of salt and pepper. Cook gently for 10 minutes.

- Blend in a food processor until smooth, then pass through a sieve. Mix the pesto sauce into the mixture thoroughly.

STUFFED COD FILLETS

Ingredients

The Cod
1 cod in 2 fillets
rind and juice of a whole lemon
150ml/ a quarter pint of white wine
salt and pepper

The Sauce
1 400g/14 oz tin tomatoes, chopped
1 small red onion
2 cloves garlic, crushed
2 tbs white wine vinegar
1 tblsp Demerara sugar
150ml/ a quarter pint of red wine

The Stuffing
225g/8 oz white breadcrumbs
1 small onion
50g/2 oz butter
1 tblsp each of parsley, thyme
and chives
rind of 1 lemon

Method

- Wash and pat dry the fish well, season with salt and pepper.

- To make the sauce: chop the onion finely. Melt the butter in a saucepan and fry the onion and garlic for 2-3 minutes. Add the breadcrumbs, herbs and lemon rind and mix well.

- Place one fillet on a piece of foil, spread the stuffing on top and place the other fillet on the stuffing.

- Brush the fillets with butter, pour the wine over them, wrap the foil tightly and bake for 15 minutes at 200C/400F/Gas 6.

- To make the tomato sauce: finely chop the onion and garlic and fry gently in a little oil, then add the tin of tomatoes, wine vinegar, red wine and sugar. Bring to the boil and simmer for 10 minutes, or until it reduces a little.

- Add the tablespoon of parsley.

- Serve the fish on a large plate with the sauce poured around it.

TIP: You can also use Hake or Haddock. The tomato sauce makes this a favourite dish for children.

STUFFED TROUT

A superb meal for a barbecue on a summer evening.

Ingredients
4 medium sized trout, cleaned, bones and fins removed, heads and tails left on

The Lemon Butter
50g/2 oz butter
2 tsp grated lemon rind
1 tbs chives and parsley, finely chopped

The Stuffing
2 tbs olive oil
1 shallot, finely chopped
1 clove garlic, crushed
50g/2 oz breadcrumbs
rind and juice of a whole lemon
2 tbs parsley, finely chopped

Method
- First prepare the lemon butter: combine all the ingredients and form a sausage shape. Wrap in foil and refrigerate.

- To make the stuffing: fry the shallots and garlic until soft.

- Add the breadcrumbs, parsley, lemon rind and juice and mix well.

- Stuff the trout with the filling and place on a fish rack over the coals. Cook for 4 minutes each side. Serve with a slice of lemon, circles of lemon butter and salad.

VEGETARIAN
MEALS

PANCAKES

Ingredients
115g/4 oz strong plain flour
pinch of salt
3 eggs
275ml/half a pint of milk
oil for frying
50g/2 oz melted butter

Method
- Place the flour in a bowl; make a well in the centre, pour the butter and eggs in and mix, gradually adding the milk.

- Beat until smooth, then leave to stand for half an hour – it will thicken slightly in this time – then pour into a jug.

- Heat a little oil in a pancake pan and pour in some of the mixture, turning the pan so that the mixture is spread evenly across the bottom.

- Cook on a medium heat until set, then turn over and cook the other side.

- Continue cooking the pancakes, placing the cooked ones on a plate and covering with foil to keep warm. Use a filling of your choice, sweet or savoury.

> *TIP: Here are some ideas for various tasty fillings:*
> - *mushrooms fried in garlic butter with soft cheese;*
> - *grated Cheddar cheese, thinly sliced ham and chives;*
> - *tuna flakes with mayonnaise and parsley;*
> - *fresh fruit and cream;*
> - *Nutella and tinned pears.*

SUMMER VEGETABLE FLANS

Ingredients
The Pastry
175g/6 oz plain flour
50g/2 oz walnuts
salt and pepper
115g/4 oz butter

The Filling
175g/6oz courgettes
1 clove garlic, crushed
175g/6 oz broccoli
50g/2 oz peas
115g/4 oz fresh tomatoes
115g/4 oz soft cheese
150ml/a quarter pint single cream
3 eggs
2 tbs fresh herbs, finely chopped
50g/2 oz mature Cheddar cheese, grated

Method
- Mix pastry ingredients in a blender with enough water to bind.

- Roll out the pastry and divide between 6 individual flan tins.

- Line the dough with pieces of foil and bake blind for 10 minutes at 200C/400F/ Gas 6.

- To prepare the filling: finely chop the courgettes and broccoli and place in a saucepan of boiling water with the peas. Boil for 5 minutes and drain.

- Place the tomatoes in boiling water for 2-3 minutes, peel and halve, and de-seed. Chop finely.

- Mix together the soft cheese, Cheddar, cream, eggs and garlic.

- Put the vegetables in the flans and pour the cheese mixture over them.

- Cook for 30 minutes at 180C/350F/Gas 4.

NUT ROAST

Ingredients
225g/8 oz mixed nuts (cashews, hazelnuts and almonds)
1 tbs olive oil
1 onion, finely chopped
2 cloves garlic, crushed
4 medium sized carrots, grated
2 medium sized courgettes, grated
115g/4 oz grated Cheddar cheese
3 tbs parsley, finely chopped
115g/4 oz wholemeal breadcrumbs
2 eggs
1 tbs sesame seeds
2 tbs thyme
salt and pepper
cucumber and dill to garnish

Method
- Grease and line a 1-pound loaf tin.

- Chop the nuts finely.

- Heat the oil and fry the onion, then add the garlic.

- Place all the other ingredients in a bowl and mix thoroughly.

- Add the onion and garlic to the other ingredients. Put it all in the tin and press down firmly, levelling the top.

- Cover with foil. Bake for 45 minutes at 180C/350F/Gas 4.

- Serve hot or cold with tomato sauce or a healthy green salad.

SIMPLE VEGETABLE CURRY

Ingredients
2 dessert apples
2 carrots
1 large onion
2 cloves garlic, crushed
1 tin butter beans
50g/2 oz sultanas
3 tbs curry paste
1 celeriac root
225g/8 oz broccoli florets
225g/8 oz button mushrooms
1 400g/14 oz tin tomatoes, chopped
570ml/1 pint of vegetable stock
2 tbs vegetable oil

Method

- Clean and prepare the vegetables into bite sized pieces.

- Leaving the skin on them, core and chop the apples.

- Heat a little oil in a large pan and fry the vegetables for 3-4 minutes.

- Add the curry paste and garlic and mix well.

- Add the apples, beans, tomatoes, sultanas and stock to the pan. Bring to the boil and simmer for 15-20 minutes.

- Serve with Basmati rice and popadoms.

LEEKS AND EGGS IN CHEESE SAUCE

This is extremely tasty, and therefore a family favourite.

Ingredients
The Leeks and Eggs
6 hard boiled eggs
1 clove garlic, crushed
450g/1 lb baby leeks
50g/2 oz butter

The Sauce
570ml/1 pint of milk
50g/2 oz butter
50g/2 oz plain flour
salt and pepper
115g/4 oz cheese of your choice, grated
parsley and chives to garnish

Method

- Cut the eggs in half.

- Cut the leeks into rings and wash thoroughly.

- Fry the onion and leeks gently in the butter for 5 minutes.

- A quick method of making the sauce: mix the flour and butter to make a paste, boil the milk and beat the paste into the milk gradually, then simmer until the sauce thickens.

- Add the salt and pepper, and the grated cheese, keeping a little for the top.

- Grease a gratin dish with butter, arrange the leeks in a layer in the bottom and place the eggs on top. Pour the sauce over the eggs, sprinkle over the remaining cheese and grill until golden.

- Garnish with chives and parsley, finely chopped.

- Serve with mashed potatoes.

STILTON AND CRANBERRY FILO PARCELS

Ingredients
75g/3 oz Stilton cheese
75g/3 oz fresh or frozen cranberries
150ml/ a quarter pint of port wine
75g/3 oz caster sugar
450g/1 lb Coxes apples
1 tsp finely chopped thyme
salt and pepper
half a teaspoon nutmeg
7 large leaves filo pastry

8 inch (21cm) baking tin

Method
- Place cranberries, port wine and sugar in a saucepan and bring slowly to the boil.

- Simmer for 10 minutes and leave to cool.

- Peel and dice the apples. Mix in the cheese, thyme and nutmeg, then add the cranberries in their juice.

- Take two leaves of filo and brush with butter. Line the tin with them, allowing to overlap the sides. Cover the remaining leaves of filo with a damp cloth or kitchen paper.

- Place half the stilton mixture on the filo. Cut the filo pieces in half, brush with butter and place on the mixture. Put the remaining mixture on this. Place another piece of filo on top. Brush with butter.

- Cook for 25 minutes at 180C/350F/Gas 4.

- Serve hot.

SUMMER COUSCOUS

This summer vegetarian dish is very healthy and colourful.

Ingredients
5 spring onions
2 yellow peppers
2 red peppers
2 cloves garlic, crushed
225g/8 oz courgettes
1 tbs mint, finely chopped
450g/1 lb shallots
1 tbs parsley, finely chopped
salt and pepper
2 tbs olive oil
1 tbs Worcestershire sauce

Method
- Chop the spring onions and clean the shallots.

- Cut the 4 peppers in half, de-seed and chop finely.

- Cut the courgettes into *julienne* strips.

- Place the *couscous* in a large bowl and cover with boiling water. Let it soak for 15 minutes, then fluff up with a fork.

- Heat the oil in a large pan and add all the vegetables, the garlic and Worcestershire sauce. Cook quickly for 5 minutes, then add the tomatoes, parsley and mint.

- Place the vegetables on a bed of *couscous* to serve.

POTATO, LEEK AND PARSNIP PATTIES

Ingredients
450g/1 lb potatoes
450g/1 lb leeks, finely chopped
450g/1 lb parsnips
75g/3 oz butter
salt, pepper and nutmeg
1 egg
115g/4 oz Parmesan cheese

Method

- Cook the potatoes and parsnips in very little water or in the microwave. Mash together.

- Cook the leeks in the butter.

- Mix the leeks with the mashed potato and parsnip, add the salt, pepper and nutmeg and bind with the egg.

- Form into 12 patties and dip in the cheese.

- Place on a greased baking tray and bake for 20 minutes at 200C/ 400F/Gas 6.

- Serve with tomato sauce (see p. 34).

SPICY POTATOES

Ingredients
675g/ a pound and a half new potatoes
pinch of salt
1 onion
1 red pepper
1 tsp *garam massala*
4 tbs curry paste
3 tbs mango chutney
450 ml/ three quarters of a pint of *passata*
1 tbs oil

Method
- Clean the potatoes thoroughly.

- Cut them in half and parboil for 10 minutes in salt water. Drain well.

- Finely chop the onion, cut the pepper in half and de-seed.

- Heat the oil in a large saucepan and fry the onion and pepper for 2-3 minutes. Add the spices and cook for a further 2 minutes.

- Add the potatoes, the chutney and the *passata* and bring to the boil, stirring occasionally.

- Cover and simmer for 15-20 minutes until the potatoes are soft.

RED AND WHITE MEATS

WINTER PORK HOTPOT

This meal is excellent for freezing.

Ingredients
900g/2 lb boned pork shoulder
450g/1 lb button onions, cleaned
2 cloves garlic, crushed
225g/8 oz carrots, diced
2 Coxes apples, diced
2 level tbs Demerara sugar
2 tbs wine vinegar
a few drops chilli sauce
1 level tbs each of thyme, parsley and oregano
1 400g/14 oz tin haricot beans
1 400g/14 oz tin tomatoes
450 ml/ three quarters of a pint of red wine
50g/2 oz butter
1 tbs olive oil

Method
- Cut the pork into 1" (2.5cm) cubes.

- Heat the oil and butter in a large oven dish or heavy saucepan.

- Fry the pork for 2-3 minutes until sealed and golden.

- Add the onions, garlic, carrots and apples, all finely chopped.

- Add the sugar, vinegar, chilli sauce, herbs, haricot beans (drained) and tomatoes, and bring to the boil.

- Cover and simmer over the heat for 40 minutes, or in the oven for 60 minutes at 180C/350F/Gas 4.

- Garnish with parsley and serve with pasta.

LEEK PARSNIP AND BACON PIE

This pie has a distinctly Welsh flavour, with the lovely combination of parsnips, leeks and bacon making it particularly tasty.

Ingredients

345g/12 oz parsnips	225g/8 oz low fat soft cheese
345g/12 oz leeks	50g/2 oz Parmesan cheese
8 leaves filo pastry	salt and pepper
50g/2 oz butter or oil	150ml/ a quarter pint of single cream
115g/4 oz boiled bacon	2 tbs parsley, finely chopped

8-10 inch (21-26cm) flan dish

Method

- Clean and cut the parsnips into bite sized pieces; clean and cut the leeks in shreds.

- Cover leeks and parsnips with cold water in a saucepan. Bring to the boil and cook for 5-7 minutes, then drain.

- Line the flan tin with 6 leaves of filo and brush with melted butter or oil between each leaf. Let the pastry overlap the sides.

- Fill with the cooked vegetables and the bacon, finely chopped.

- Mix together the cream, soft cheese and parsley and pour over the filling.

- Fold the overlapping pastry over the top and cover with the two remaining leaves, brushing with the last of the butter or oil.

- Bake for 30 minutes at 180C/350F/Gas 4.

- Serve with salad.

TIP: Waste not, want not – don't throw the vegetable stock away, use it to make soup.

HONEY ROAST HAM WITH A FRUITY SAUCE

Baking your own ham is very easy, and the difference in taste and the wonderful aroma in your kitchen is well worth the extra effort. Picture your ham in its colourful covering of honey, orange juice and Demerara sugar, on a large plate and garnished with orange slices and watercress!

Ingredients
The Ham
900g/2 lb gammon joint
1 tsp mustard
12 cloves
50g/2 oz Demerara sugar
2 tbs honey
3 tbs orange juice

The Sauce
3 tbs redcurrant jelly
rind and juice of 1 orange
3 tbs orange juice
rind and juice of 1 lemon
150ml/ a quarter pint of ham stock **or**
150ml/ a quarter pint of red wine
slices of orange to garnish

Method
- Soak the gammon joint in cold water overnight. Then place the gammon in a large saucepan, cover with cold water, bring to the boil, remove the foam (which is the salt) and simmer for 30 minutes.

- Remove the joint from the saucepan and carefully strip off the skin. Score the fat with a sharp knife and stud with cloves. Place on a baking tray.

- Blend together the sugar, honey, mustard and orange juice and pour over the gammon.

- Cook in a moderate oven for 45 minutes at 180C/350F/Gas 4.

- While the meat is cooking, prepare the sauce by combining the ingredients, and boil together for 10 minutes.

- Take the joint out of the oven and spoon the glaze juices over it. Cook on high at 220C/425F/Gas 7 for a further 15-20 minutes until you have a lovely glaze.

- Serve with the sauce for that special Sunday lunch.

ORANGE AND HONEY CHICKEN

A marinade of orange juice and honey gives the chicken a wonderful sweetness that caramelises the chicken.

Ingredients
4 skinless chicken breasts
2 tbs soy sauce
2 tbs honey
1 tbs wholegrain mustard
salt and pepper
1 clove garlic, crushed
orange slices, rindless

Method
- Cut a pocket in the side of each chicken breast and fill with orange slices.

- Mix together the remaining ingredients to make the marinade and pour over the chicken breasts. Leave for one hour.

- Place the chicken and the marinade in a roasting dish and place in a hot oven at 200C/400F/Gas 6 for 30 minutes, or until the chicken is cooked.

- Serve with roast potatoes, baby carrots and mixed beans.

CHICKEN MARENGO

This is a traditional French dish – it is very tasty, and a particular favourite of presenter Alwyn Humphreys.

Ingredients
4 skinless chicken breasts
50g/2 oz cornflour
150ml/ a quarter pint of olive oil
50g/2 oz butter
1 onion, sliced
4 tbs brandy
salt and pepper
450g/1 lb tomatoes, skinned or 1 400g/14 oz tin tomatoes, chopped
2 cloves garlic, crushed
150ml/ a quarter pint of chicken stock
115g/4 oz button mushrooms

Method
- Toss the chicken in the cornflour.

- Heat the oil in a large frying pan, and fry the chicken for 5-10 minutes each side. Remove from the pan and set aside.

- Sprinkle the brandy and salt and pepper over the chicken breasts. To the frying pan, add the onions and cook for 3 minutes.

- Add the tomatoes, garlic and stock.

- Put the chicken back in the sauce, cover and simmer for 30 minutes.

- If you prefer to use the oven, place the chicken and the sauce in a casserole dish in the oven at 180C/350F/Gas 4 for 45 minutes.

- Cook the mushrooms in butter for 3-4 minutes, then add to the chicken before serving.

- Serve hot with vegetables of your choice.

Tomato, Cucumber and Caerphilly Cheese Salad
(see page 11)

Trout with Herb and Nut Stuffing
(see page 27)

Summer Vegetable Flans
(see page 40)

Fillet Steak on Mustard Croutons
(see page 64)

Ena's Gift Ideas
(see pages 69-79)

Venison Sausages with Pepper Stir Fry
(see page 88)

Bread and Cakes
(see pages 89-102)

Treacle Pudding
(see page 110)

STUFFED CHICKEN BREASTS IN A WINE SAUCE

Ingredients
The Chicken
4 skinless chicken breasts
150ml/ a quarter pint of red wine

The Filling
115g/4 oz smoked back bacon, cooked
75g/3 oz mushrooms
115g/4 oz ready-to-eat apricots, finely chopped
115g/4 oz white breadcrumbs
2 tbs fresh herbs, finely chopped; basil, thyme and parsley
salt and pepper
rind and juice 2 lemons
50g/2 oz walnuts
olive oil
1 egg
arrowroot to thicken

Method
- Place the chicken breasts between two sheets of clingfilm and pat with a rolling pin.

- Mix all the filling ingredients together and bind with the egg.

- Put a little filling on each chicken breast and roll tightly, securing with cocktail sticks.

- Heat the olive oil in a frying pan until spitting. Place the chicken in the hot oil and fry until golden – 5 minutes each side should be fine.

- Pour the wine into the mixture, cover and cook for 15-20 minutes.

- If necessary, thicken the sauce by adding some arrowroot mixed with water.

- Serve with vegetables or salad.

> **TIP:** *You can freeze the chicken, but it must be taken out of the freezer and defrosted for 10 hours before serving.*

STUFFED LOIN OF LAMB

This is one of my personal favourites, Welsh lamb, sweet, tender and delicious.

Ingredients
900g/2 lb loin of lamb

The Stuffing
1 onion, finely chopped
225g/8 oz white breadcrumbs
50g/2 oz melted butter or oil
rind 1 orange
225g/8 oz pineapple, finely chopped
1 tbs parsley, finely chopped
1 tsp thyme, finely chopped
115g/4 oz pork sausagemeat

Method
- Take the skin off the lamb, and bone.

- Cook the onion in a little oil.

- Place the onion and all the other ingredients of the stuffing in a large bowl, and mix well to bind.

- Place the stuffing in the middle of the loin and roll the meat up around it. Tie with string at 1-inch (2.5cm) intervals. Cut the loin between the string.

- Fry in hot oil for 3 minutes each side.

- Serve with glazed onions and green vegetables.

SIZZLING TENDERLOIN OF LAMB WITH CRANBERRY AND APPLE SAUCE

A mouth-watering method of serving lamb, which is simple – yet effective!

Ingredients
450g/1 lb lamb tenderloin
1 tbs olive oil

The Sauce
225g/8 oz fresh or frozen cranberries
450 ml/ three quarters of a pint of apple juice
rind and juice 1 orange
2 tbs clear honey

Method
- Brush the loin with oil and place under a hot grill for 4-5 minutes, turning to make sure cooking and browning on both sides. The lamb should be crisp outside and pink inside.

- To make the sauce, place all the ingredients in a saucepan and simmer for 10 minutes.

- Cut the meat into thick slices; pour a little of the sauce around the slices, and serve with fresh vegetables of your choice.

SPICY LAMB WITH PILAU RICE

Ingredients
The Meat
450g/1 lb leg of lamb, cubed in 1-inch(2.5 cm) pieces
2 cloves garlic, crushed
1 large onion, sliced
1 inch (2.5 cm) ginger root, finely chopped
2 small hot chilli peppers, finely chopped
1 handful fresh coriander
1 tsp ground cumin
1 tsp ground turmeric
rind and juice 1 lime
275ml/half a pint of vegetable stock
150ml/ a quarter pint of natural yoghurt
25g/1 oz almond flakes
arrowroot to thicken

The Rice
225g/8 oz long grain rice
2 cloves garlic, crushed
1 small onion, finely chopped
2 tbs olive oil
570ml/1 pint of water or vegetable stock

Method
- Heat a little oil in a large pan and quickly fry the lamb until evenly browned, remove from the pan and set aside.

- Add the garlic, onion, chilli peppers and all the spices to the pan and cook for 5 minutes.

- Add the stock, bring to the boil and put the meat in the sauce.

- Cover and simmer for one hour, then thicken the sauce with 2 teaspoons of arrowroot and the yoghurt.

- To prepare the rice, heat a little oil in a saucepan, fry the onion and garlic for 2-3 minutes. Add the rice and stock, cover and boil until the rice has absorbed the liquid.

- Serve the lamb on the rice, and garnish with slices of cucumber, banana and tomato, and fresh coriander.

EASY LAMB BURGERS

A childrens' favourite because they're so tasty – and they're healthy, which keeps the parents happy!

Ingredients
450g/1 lb minced lamb
1 small onion, finely chopped
1 dessert apple, grated
2 spring onions, finely chopped
1 tbs brandy
a few drops Tabasco sauce
1 clove garlic, crushed
1 tsp wholegrain mustard
115g/4 oz white breadcrumbs
1 tbs tomato *purée*
salt and pepper
1 beaten egg
50g/2 oz plain flour
4 tbs olive oil

Method
- Mix all the ingredients together, and bind with the beaten egg.

- Divide into 8 portions and shape into burgers.

- Fry in hot oil for 2-3 minutes each side.

TIP: You can use chicken, turkey or pork instead of lamb.

FILLET STEAK ON MUSTARD *CROUTONS*

Ingredients
The Steak
2 175g/6 oz fillet steaks
2 slices bacon
2 slices bread, cut in circles
2 tsp butter
1 tsp wholegrain mustard
oil for frying

The Filling
50g/2 oz butter
4 shallots, finely chopped
50g/2 oz mushrooms
1 clove garlic, crushed
50g/2 oz white breadcrumbs
lemon rind

Method
- To prepare the filling: fry the shallots, mushrooms and garlic in the butter.

- Cut a pocket in the side of each steak and fill with the mushroom mixture.

- Wrap each steak in bacon and secure with a cocktail stick.

- Spread the circles of bread with butter and mustard and grill both sides.

- Fry the steaks quickly in butter and hot oil until well browned on each side.

- Serve with asparagus and buttered carrots.

PAN FRIED STEAK WITH MUSHROOM AND CREAM SAUCE

Ingredients
4 175g/6 oz sirloin steaks
4 small shallots
olive oil
4 tbs mustard
3 cloves garlic, crushed
salt and pepper
8 tbs brandy
275ml/half a pint of single cream
175g/6 oz mushrooms

Method

- Finely chop the shallots.

- Pour a little oil into a heavy pan. Heat the pan and when very hot fry the meat (see below). Place the steaks on a hot plate and keep in a low oven.

- To make the sauce: add the shallots, mustard, garlic, brandy and mushrooms to the same pan with 4 tablespoons water.

- Bring to the boil and reduce slightly, then add the cream and bring back to the boil. Season to taste.

- Serve the steaks on the *croutons* and pour some sauce over each steak.

- Serve with fresh salad and new potatoes.

TIP: Here are some handy timings for steak cooked to different tastes:
Rare: 2.5 minutes per side
Medium: 3.5 minutes each side
Well done: 6 minutes each side

SPICY CHRISTMAS CASSEROLE

A delicious casserole, ideal for freezing for Boxing Day or New Year's Day.

Ingredients
450g/1 lb stewing steak
450g/1 lb venison
225g/8 oz ready-to-eat apricots
115g/4 oz raisins
275ml/half a pint of fresh orange juice
175ml/6 fl oz dry sherry **or** port wine
salt and pepper
450g/1 lb small onions
2 tbs olive oil
2 tsp allspice
570ml/1 pint of beef stock
2 tbs raspberry vinegar
1 tbs Demerara
1 orange

Method
- Cut the meat into cubes and marinade overnight in the sherry or port.

- Strain the meat the following day, keeping the liquid for stock. Heat the oil in a large pan and fry the meat to seal those lovely juices.

- Place the meat in a casserole dish.

- Fry the onions in the pan for 2-3 minutes, add the raisins, sugar, sherry stock, and the rind and juice of the orange.

- Bring them back to the boil, pour the sauce over the meat and cook for 2 hours at 180C/350F/Gas 4.

- Serve with *couscous* and fruit.

GIFTS IDEAS
FROM ENA

STRAWBERRY ICE-CREAM

This is a truly summery ice-cream, made from strawberries straight off the plant.

Ingredients
3 egg yolks
75g/3 oz caster sugar
275ml/ half a pint of milk
275ml/ half a pint of double cream
450g/1 lb strawberries
2 tsp cornflour

Method
- Whisk together yolks, sugar and cornflour until white and creamy.
- Heat the milk to simmering point and pour over the yolks and sugar. Blend well.
- Pour the custard into the rinsed pan and heat until it coats the back of a wooden spoon.
- Pour into a bowl, cover with clingfilm and leave to cool.
- Whisk the double cream until it thickens, then fold into the custard.
- Purée the strawberries, then sieve to remove the seeds.
- Fold the *purée* into the custard. Pour into a freezer container and freeze for 2-3 hours. Remove from the freezer and whisk thoroughly to break down the ice crystals. Return to the freezer for 2-3 hours.
- If the ice-cream has been in the freezer for 24 hours, transfer to the fridge for 15 minutes before serving.

> *TIP: If you're giving the ice-cream as a gift, place the ice-cream container in a freezer bag or thick layers of newspaper to carry it without it defrosting. A ribbon around the box and a hand-made label makes the gift even more special.*

MAYONNAISE

Ingredients
1 whole egg **or** 2 egg yolks
a quarter tsp mustard powder
half a tsp salt
1-2 tbs wine vinegar **or** lemon juice
275ml/ half a pint of olive oil
1 tbs boiling water

Method using a Blender
- Using a blender, put the egg in with the mustard, salt, vinegar or lemon juice, and run the machine on low power for around 3 minutes until smoothly blended.

- While operating the machine, add the oil in a slow, steady stream, followed by the boiling water until the mayonnaise is perfectly blended.

Method by Hand
- To make mayonnaise by hand, place a small bowl on a folded cloth to prevent it slipping.

- Put the egg in the bowl with the mustard, salt and a few drops of vinegar or lemon juice. Using a small wire whisk or hand-held electric beater, whisk thoroughly before adding the oil.

- Keep beating and start adding the oil drop by drop from a tea-spoon, continuing until the sauce thickens and half the oil has been added.

- Add a teaspoon of vinegar or lemon juice and, still beating, add the remaining oil to the mixture in a steady flow.

- When all the oil has been incorporated, and the mayonnaise is thick, beat in the boiling water and season to taste using the remaining vinegar or lemon juice.

GIFT IDEA: Try and find unusual jars in kitchen shops and second-hand shops, and decorate as creatively as you like!

TIP: Here are some different recipes to vary the kinds of mayonnaise you can make :

- **CHANTILLY MAYONNAISE**

  Use lemon juice instead of vinegar, and fold 4-5 table-spoons of whipped double cream into the mayonnaise.

- **SAUCE *TARTARE***

  To the mayonnaise, add 1-2 tablespoons gherkins, finely chopped, and chopped capers, chives and parsley.

- ***REMOULADE* SAUCE**

  To the Sauce *Tartare*, add a teaspoon each of mustard and anchovy sauce.

- **SEAFOOD COCKTAIL SAUCE**

  Mix 6 level tablespoons mayonnaise with a tablespoon each of tomato ketchup and soured cream or double cream, and season to taste with a few drops of Worcestershire sauce and lemon juice.

- **GARLIC MAYONNAISE**

  Pound 2 peeled garlic cloves to a fine paste and add to the egg yolks as you start a hand mixed mayonnaise. Not advisable for a blender mayonnaise.

CHOCOLATE FRUIT CRUNCH

Ingredients
450g/1 lb milk chocolate, broken into pieces
175g/6 oz unsalted butter
275ml/ half a pint of double cream
450g/1 lb Digestive biscuits, crushed
115g/4 oz raisins
115g/4 oz walnuts
115g/4 oz *glacé* cherries

Method

- Melt the chocolate and butter in a bowl over a saucepan of simmering water.

- Remove from the heat, pour in the double cream and mix well.

- Stir in the broken biscuits, raisins, nuts and halved cherries.

- Pour the mixture into a Swiss roll tin lined with clingfilm and leave to set for 3-4 hours, then cut into small squares; or pour the mixture directly into *petit four* cases.

> *TIP: It is not advisable to melt the chocolate in the microwave as it could burn easily.*

GIFT IDEA: This Crunch makes a great Christmas present, packed in a pretty box with a ribbon bow. If it is intended for adults, a tablespoon of brandy is lovely in the mixture.

LEMON CURD

Ingredients
6 lemons
450g/1 lb caster sugar
6 Size 3 eggs
175g/6 oz unsalted butter

Method
- Scrub and dry the lemons and grate the rind finely.
- Cut the lemons in half, squeeze out all the juice and place in a large bowl with the rind.
- Add the sugar to the bowl, beat the eggs thoroughly and place in the bowl with the butter.
- Place the bowl over a pan of simmering water, stirring until the sugar melts. Continue to cook until the curd thickens enough to cover the back of a wooden spoon.
- Pour into sterilised jars, cover with waxed paper circles and leave to cool before sealing.
- Store in the fridge for up to one month.

TIP 1: *Mix 1 tablespoon of the lemon curd into 275ml/ half a pint of natural yoghurt and freeze – delicious in the summer.*

TIP 2: *To make a special lemon sponge, beat 275ml/ half a pint of double cream and fold in 2 tablespoons of the lemon curd. Spread between two sponges.*

GIFT IDEA: Choose a plain jar to show off the glorious colour, and cover the lid with coloured material and a ribbon.

CHRISTMAS RUM TRUFFLES

Ingredients
75g/3 oz plain sweet biscuits, crushed
2 tbs *glacé* cherries, finely chopped
2 tbs hazelnuts, finely chopped
2 tbs ground almonds
2 tbs raisins, chopped
1 tbs rum **or** brandy
a few drops vanilla essence
50g/2 oz butter
175g/6 oz plain chocolate
2 tbs thick double cream
nuts or *vermicelli* to coat

Method

- Melt the butter and chocolate together in the microwave on full power for 1 minute or in a bowl over a saucepan of water.

- Place the biscuits, cherries, nuts, raisins and rum (or brandy) in a bowl.

- Pour the chocolate and cream in, and mix well. Leave to cool in the fridge for 30 minutes.

- Mould into 40 truffles and dip each one in the nuts or *vermicelli.*

GIFT IDEA: Put the truffles in pretty paper cases in an old-fashioned tin or a box decorated with wrapping paper and ribbon.

BRANDY MINCEMEAT

This is a fabulous recipe, and makes a change from the usual Christmas mince-meat. You'll be surprised at how easy it is to prepare, and it tastes wonderful.

Ingredients
250g/9 oz apricots
250g/9 oz pears
250g/9 oz apple chunks } use dried fruit,
250g/9 oz peaches soaked overnight
225g/8 oz walnuts, finely chopped
225g/8 dark Muscovado sugar
2 tsps allspice
175g/6 oz melted butter
275ml/half a pint of brandy

Method
- Chop all the fruit finely and mix in allspice and walnuts.

- Melt the butter in the microwave or in a bowl over a saucepan of water.

- Add the melted butter to the fruit and pour in the brandy. Stir well.

- Store in sterilised jars for a month or two.

> **TIP: For a special dessert, make a large pastry case, or filo parcels filled with the mincemeat.**

GIFT IDEA: Decorate the jar according to taste.

PICKLES

These make excellent presents for friends and family at Christmas. Use jars with coloured lids. You can pick these up without spending too much.

PICKLED PEACHES/PEARS
2kg/4 lb peaches/pears
570ml/1 pint white spiced vinegar

Method
- Peel the fruit, then halve and quarter, removing the stone or centre.
- Heat the vinegar and poach the fruit in it for 10 minutes until tender.
- Pack the fruit tightly in warm, clean jars.
- Boil the syrup rapidly for 2-3 minutes to reduce.
- Pour the syrup over the fruit. Seal immediately.

PICKLED ONIONS
1.35kg/4 lb small pickling onions
570ml/1 pint white spiced vinegar

Method
- To make the onions easier to peel, pour boiling water over them and allow to cool.
- After peeling them, cover with salt for 24 hours, then wash off the salt. Pack tightly into clean jars and cover with cold pickling vinegar.
- Seal and leave for a month or two. If you're late pickling, you can leave them for just two weeks, but no less than that, or they'll be quite tasteless!

PICKLED EGGS

6 hard boiled eggs
570ml/1 pint white spiced vinegar
2 bay leaves

Method

- Place the eggs in a clean jar, pour the vinegar over them and add the bay leaves.
- Seal immediately and leave for at least a fortnight before eating.

PICKLED RED CABBAGE

1 large red cabbage
1.8 l/3 pints white spiced vinegar

Method

- Choose a firm, brightly coloured cabbage.
- Remove outer leaves and centre stalk.
- Shred the cabbage finely, layer with salt in a large bowl and leave for 24 hours.
- Drain and wash off the salt. Pack the cabbage loosely in jars, cover with cold vinegar and seal.
- Leave for a month before eating.

PICKLED BEETROOT

1.35kg/3 lbs cooked beetroot
570ml/1 pint white spiced vinegar

Method

- Peel the beetroot and cut into cubes or slices.
- Pack into clean jars and cover with cold vinegar.
- Seal and leave for at least a fortnight before eating.
- To add a special taste to the beetroot, finely chop a small red onion into the jars.

THREE FRUIT MARMALADE

Nothing beats the taste of home-made marmalade. It's worth every ounce of effort you put into it.

Ingredients
450g/1 lb sweet oranges (2 oranges)
450g/1 lb ripe lemons (4 lemons)
700g/ a pound and a half ruby red grapefruit (2 fruits)
2.7kg/7 lb jam sugar with pectin
2.8l/5 pints water

Method
- Scrub the fruit and dry well.

- With a fruit zester, remove all the skin off each fruit. Using a zester makes thin cut marmalade.

- If you prefer thick cut marmalade, peel the fruit and chop according to taste.

- Cut each fruit in half and squeeze out all the juice. Wrap all the pips in a piece of muslin with a little zest.

- Put the peel, juice and cold water in a large preserving pan, with the pips and zest in the muslin; bring to the boil and boil until it reduces by half, and the peel is cooked.

- Pour the sugar in slowly and stir until it dissolves, then boil until you have a 'rolling boil' for about 30 minutes.

- To test the jam, pour a little onto a cold saucer from the fridge. If it forms a wrinkle while still tepid, the marmalade should be set.

- Leave the marmalade to cool in the pan, this makes it easier to pot. Make sure the jars are very clean and dry. Cover with wax discs then cellophane. Label and store in a cool place for up to 6 months.

GAME

GOOSE FEAST WITH APRICOT STUFFING

Ingredients
a 4.5kg/10 lb goose
225g/8 oz ready-to-eat apricots
juice and rind 1 lemon
345g/12 oz white breadcrumbs
2 onions, finely chopped
2 cooking apples, finely chopped
1 tbs dried sage
1 tbs fresh parsley
1 yellow pepper and 1 red pepper, de-seeded and roughly chopped
115g/4 oz melted butter
2 eggs, beaten

Method
- Remove the giblets and wishbone from the goose, and keep the giblets to make stock for gravy.

- Cut the fatty skin away from the neck and prick the goose all over with a fork.

- Mix together all the ingredients of the stuffing and bind with the beaten egg. Use a little of the stuffing to fill the neck and truss loosely.

- Place the remaining stuffing on some foil and make a parcel shaped like the goose. Place the parcel in the cavity of the goose and open the foil so that the stuffing flavours the goose while cooking.

- Sprinkle with salt and place the goose on a wire rack over a roasting pan. Cook at 220C/425F/Gas 7 for 40 minutes, then reduce heat to 180C/350F/Gas 4 for 2 hours.

- Transfer to a serving dish and garnish with grapes and mint.

DUCK AND CRANBERRY TERRINE

Ingredients
450g/1 lb boneless duck breast pieces
450g/1 lb pork steaks
2 tbs brandy
1 egg
half a teaspoon nutmeg
75g/3 oz white breadcrumbs
salt and pepper
175g/6 oz fresh cranberries
2 tbs parsley

Method
- Trim any fat off the duck and pork.

- Chop finely, or process for a few seconds.

- Transfer to a large bowl and beat in the brandy, egg, nutmeg and breadcrumbs. Add salt and plenty of pepper.

- Grease and line a 900g/2 lb loaf tin.

- Press half the mixture into the tin.

- Place 115g/4 oz cranberries on top. Spoon remaining meat on top of the fruit. Press down well.

- Cover with foil and cook for 2 hours at 160C/325F/Gas 3.

- Remove from tin, garnish with cranberries and serve with brown toast.

DUCK BREASTS WITH APPLE, PLUM AND HONEY SAUCE

Ingredients
450g/1 lb duck breast fillets
3 tbs clear honey
225g/8 oz red plums
150ml/ a quarter pint of wine
150ml/ a quarter pint of apple juice
salt and pepper

Method

- Using a sharp knife, score the skin of the duck. Rub with salt and pepper.

- Preheat a heavy flameproof pan. Place the breasts, skin down, over a medium heat; cook for 7-8 minutes. Turn and cook for a further 3-4 minutes.

- The duck should be pink inside, but if you prefer it well done allow more time.

- Transfer the duck to a serving plate and keep warm. Remove all the fat from the pan, add the wine, apple juice, plums and salt and pepper to season, and bring to the boil until it reduces a little.

- Pour the sauce around the duck on a large plate and garnish with watercress.

- Serve with a medley of stir-fried spring vegetables and diced potatoes cooked in butter and oil.

GUINEA FOWL WITH GRAPES AND MADEIRA WINE

Ingredients
2 guinea fowl
2 shallots, chopped
50g/2 oz butter
1 tbs olive oil
2 oranges
175ml Madeira wine
570ml/1 pint chicken or vegetable stock
350g/12 oz seedless grapes
40g/ an ounce and a half of cornflour
2 tbs parsley, finely chopped
1 225g/8 oz tin water chestnuts

Method

- Cut each fowl into 4 portions – 2 breasts and 2 legs.

- Heat the oil and fry the meat until browned on each side.

- Move to a casserole dish.

- Clean and fry the shallots until soft.

- Add the rind and juice of the oranges, wine, stock and salt and pepper and boil gently.

- Pour the sauce over the meat and put in the oven for 1 hour at 180C/350F/Gas 4.

- Add the chestnuts and grapes and cook for a further 15 minutes.

- Remove from the oven and arrange the meat on a plate. Thicken the sauce with the cornflour mixed with water.

- Pour the sauce over the meat and garnish with the parsley.

TIP: This is marvellous with roast potatoes and parsnips, with steamed broccoli.

CHRISTMAS PHEASANT

This is a perfect dish to freeze for Christmas.

Ingredients

1 brace oven-ready pheasants
225g/8 oz streaky bacon
225g/8 oz small onions
salt and pepper
a little olive oil
50g/2 oz butter
2 cloves garlic, crushed
270ml/10 fl oz Madeira wine
570ml/1 pint leek stock

1 tsp mixed herbs
8 juniper berries
1 orange
275ml/ half a pint of redcurrant
   jelly
225g/8 oz fresh cranberries
225g/8 oz cooked chestnuts
1 tbs cornflour

Method

- Joint both pheasant into four, discarding back bone and knuckles.

- Heat the oil and butter in a large frying pan, and fry the pheasant until the meat is sealed on both sides. Move to a casserole dish.

- In the same pan, fry the onions, juniper berries, garlic and bacon for 2-3 minutes, then add to the casserole dish.

- Cover and cook in the oven for 1 hour at 180C/350F/Gas 4.

- Add the chestnuts, cranberries and redcurrant jelly to the casserole dish and cook for a further 30 minutes until the pheasant is quite tender.

- Transfer the pheasant to a plate, and if necessary, thicken the sauce again with a little cornflour mixed with water.

VENISON SAUSAGES WITH PEPPER STIR FRY

Venison sausages are extremely tasty, and give a rich flavour to this dish.

Ingredients
8 venison sausages
225g/8 oz smoked bacon
2 tblsps olive oil
2 onions
225g/8 oz button mushrooms
2 sticks celery
1 green pepper
1 red pepper
2 red apples
275ml/ half a pint of red wine

Method
- Cut the onion into rings. Wipe the mushrooms with a damp cloth.

- De-seed the two peppers and chop finely.

- Cut the celery and apple into chunks (size according to taste).

- Heat the oil in a large frying pan.

- Add the sausages, bacon and onion and cook until the sausages are brown.

- Pour away any excess fat, and add the celery, mushrooms, apples and the two peppers.

- Cook for 5 minutes, add the wine and simmer for a further 10 minutes.

- Garnish with parsley and serve with rice, pasta or potatoes.

BREAD
AND
CAKES

BASIC WHITE OR BROWN BREAD

Home-made bread is both delicious and healthy, and the smell of it baking in the house makes everyone's mouth water.

Ingredients
900g/2 lb plain strong white or brown flour
1 tsp salt
1 tsp caster sugar
25g/1 oz fresh yeast or 1 sachet easy blend dried yeast
1 tbs olive oil
570ml/1 pint (approx.) tepid water
1 beaten egg or milk, to glaze
fat to grease
sesame seeds

Method
- Sift flour and salt into a large warm bowl.

- Mix the fresh yeast with a spoonful of sugar. Make a well in the flour and pour in the oil, yeast and water (you may need more water if using wholegrain flour).

- Knead thoroughly to make a strong, soft dough, using more flour to knead. Knead for about 5 minutes to make sure the yeast is spread evenly through the flour.

- Cover the bowl with a cloth or place in a plastic bag, and leave to ride for 30 minutes. Knead again until smooth and elastic. Cut in half to make two loaves.

- Place in greased tins or moulds of your choice. Leave in a warm place to rise until the dough has risen just above the tops of the tins.

- Brush with egg or milk and sprinkle sesame seeds on top.

- Bake the bread in a hot oven for about 20-25 minutes at 220C/425F/Gas 7.

- To test if ready, take the loaf from the tin and tap the bottom. If ready, it will sound hollow. If not, replace in the tin for a further 5 minutes.

BACON AND HERB BREAD

Ingredients
225g/8 oz self-raising flour
salt and pepper
1 tsp mixed herbs
1 beaten egg
8 tbs milk
115g/4 oz streaky bacon
50g/2 oz butter
fat to grease

Method

- Place the flour, salt and pepper in a bowl. Rub in the butter. Add the herbs and cooked bacon.

- Beat the eggs and milk together and mix it all together to make a smooth dough.

- Turn the dough out on a floured board and knead lightly to make a round shape.

- Place the dough in a greased loaf tin. Score at 6 regular intervals. Bake for 10-15 minutes at 230C/450F/Gas 8.

- Cut in scored grooves when cooked and eat hot or cold.

PUFF PASTRY

Ingredients
450g/1 lb strong flour
225g/8 oz margarine or butter
225g/8 oz vegetarian fat (Trex)
juice of 1 lemon made up with water to 270ml/10 fl oz

Method
- Place the flour in a large bowl.

- Mix together fat and butter.

- Add the fat and butter to the flour in walnut-sized pieces. Gently cover the pieces with flour, using your hands.

- Add the water and lemon juice. Use a palette knife or your hands to bind together lightly.

- Using plenty of flour, roll into an oblong shape, fold the end closest to you into the middle and the far end over it. Press the sides down well. Turn the dough around and fold to your right. Repeat four times, and leave to cool for a couple of hours.

- Use as required to make sweet or savoury pies, cream horns or corned beef pasties and sausage rolls.

- Cook at 200C/400F/Gas 6 for 15-20 minutes, adjusting for filling.

STRAWBERRY AND CREAM SLICES

Ingredients
450g/1 lb puff pastry dough
570ml/1 pint double cream, beaten
450g/1 lb strawberries
icing sugar

Method

- Cut the dough in half.

- Roll each half into 8" (20cm) by 4" (10cm) wide shapes. Place onto a baking tray, using a sharp knife to score the dough in four parts. This will make it easier to cut after baking.

- Bake the dough in a hot oven at 220C/425F/Gas 7 for 15-20 minutes. It should be puffed and golden brown in colour.

- Sandwich two slices together with strawberries and cream in the middle.

- Dust with icing sugar and garnish with a sprig of mint.

BASIC SWEET SCONE MIXTURE

Ingredients
The Scones
225g/8 oz self-raising flour
1 tsp baking powder
50g/2 oz caster sugar
50g/2 oz butter
150ml/ a quarter pint of milk
1 beaten egg or milk, to glaze

The Filling
275ml/ half a pint of double
cream
225g/8 oz raspberries

Method
- Sieve flour, salt and baking powder into a large bowl.

- Rub in the butter to resemble fine breadcrumbs.

- Mix to a firm, soft dough with the milk and lemon juice. Knead lightly and roll out to a three-quarter inch (2 cm) thickness before cutting into rounds or making one large scone.

- Place on a greased baking tray and cook for 10-15 minutes at 200C/400F/Gas 6.

- When cooked and cooled, split scones in half and fill with cream and raspberries.

TIP: Here are some ideas to vary the basic recipe.
Prepare the mixture as above and add
the ingredients on page 97.

APRICOT AND WALNUT SCONES

Basic scone mixture
50g/2 oz ready-to-eat apricots
50g/2 oz walnuts

CHERRY SCONES

Basic scone mixture
50g/2 oz cherries, finely chopped

BASIC SAVOURY SCONE MIX

Ingredients
225g/8 oz self-raising flour
1 tsp baking powder
half a teaspoon salt
half a teaspoon lemon juice
150ml/ a quarter pint of milk or buttermilk
50g/2 oz butter

Method
- Sieve flour, salt and baking powder into a large bowl.

- Rub in the butter to resemble fine breadcrumbs.

- Mix to a firm, soft dough with the milk and lemon juice. Knead lightly and roll out to a three-quarter inch (2 cm) thickness before cutting into rounds or making one large scone.

- Place on a greased baking tray and cook for 10-15 minutes at 200C/400F/Gas 6.

PIZZA

Pizza originated in Italy, where women would make bread and keep a piece of dough, making a round shape of it and baking with tomato, onions and cheese on top.

Pizza today is more sophisticated, and can be a great main course as well as a snack.

Basic Pizza Dough
225g/8 oz strong plain flour
half a teaspoon salt
25g/1 oz fresh yeast **or** 1 sachet easy blend yeast
3 tbs olive oil
warm water

Basic Tomato Sauce
1 400g/14 oz tin chopped tomatoes
1 onion, finely chopped
2 tbs tomato *purée*
1 clove garlic, crushed
1 tsp mixed herbs
1 glass white wine

Method
- Mix the flour, salt and yeast in a bowl. Add 2 tablespoons of olive oil and about 6 fluid ounces of warm water to make a soft but not sticky dough.

- Turn out onto a floured surface and knead.

- Roll out to a 20" (26 cm) round and place on a greased baking tray.

- Cover and leave to rise while making the topping. When the dough has risen, brush with oil and spread the topping over it. Bake in a hot oven at 220C/425F/Gas 7 for 15-20 minutes.

- To make the topping, place all the ingredients in a saucepan and boil quickly for 10 minutes. Spread over the dough.

TIP: You can be as traditional or as adventurous as you like when choosing toppings for your pizza. Here are some ideas.

CARMARTHEN HAM, LEEK AND GRAPE
1 400g/14 oz tin chopped tomatoes
225g/8 oz Mozzarella cheese
450g/1 lb Carmarthen ham
2 small leeks
175g/6 oz seedless grapes
1 tsp mixed herbs
1 glass white wine
1 clove garlic, crushed

VEGETARIAN
1 220g/7 oz tin tomatoes
half an onion, finely chopped
1 tsp tomato *purée*
1 clove garlic, crushed
175g/6 oz mushrooms
175g/6 oz broccoli florets
175g/6 oz Cheddar cheese

SEAFOOD

basic tomato sauce
1 small tin tuna
150ml/ a quarter pint of cockles **or** 115g/4 oz prawns
2 tbs olive oil
1 clove garlic, crushed
1 bunch spring onions
2 tbs fresh parsley

SALAMI AND PINEAPPLE

basic tomato sauce
175g/6 oz selection of sliced salami
50g/2 oz Parma ham
175g/6 oz Parmesan cheese
225g/8 oz fresh pineapple, finely chopped

ENA'S WELSH CAKES (*PICE BACH*)

Ingredients
225g/8 oz self-raising flour
115g/4 oz butter
115g/4 oz caster sugar
1 tsp vanilla essence
2 eggs
a drop of milk
75g/3 oz sultanas

Method
- Rub the butter into the flour until it resembles fine bread-crumbs. Add the sugar and sultanas.

- Beat the eggs and add to the crumbs with the vanilla essence and milk to make a soft, but firm dough.

- Sprinkle some flour on the dough and roll out to a quarter inch (1 cm) thickness before cutting into 2" (5 cm) rounds and cooking on a hot griddle for 2-3 minutes each side.

ALMOND APPLE TART

This apple tart is slightly different, with the almond taste adding to the unusual flavour.

Ingredients
The Crust
225g/8 oz self-raising flour
115g/4 oz white fat
50g/2 oz caster sugar
1 egg yolk
a little water to bind

The Filling
450g/1 lb cooking apples, peeled and
   finely chopped
1 tsp lemon juice
1 tbs apricot jam
50g/2 oz ground almonds
a quarter teaspoon allspice
115g/4 oz caster sugar

Method
- Rub the fat into the flour.

- Add the sugar and mix well.

- Bind with the egg yolk and 2-3 tablespoons of cold water.

- Divide the dough in half, and roll out one half to cover an 8" (21 cm) ovenproof plate.

- Mix the ingredients of the filling together and spread over the dough. Roll out the remaining dough to the same size and place over the apples.

- Seal the edges and cut away any dough which overlaps the plate with the palms of your hands, **not** a knife. This will stop the pastry shrinking.

- Brush with egg white and dust a little sugar over the tart.

- Bake for 20-25 minutes at 200C/400F/Gas 6.

DESSERTS

BLACK FOREST CHOCOLATE ROLL

Ingredients
The Sponge
3 eggs
75g/3 oz caster sugar
75g/3 oz self-raising flour
1 tbs chocolate powder

The Filling
1 450g/1 lb tin black cherries
2 tsps arrowroot
275ml/ half a pint of double cream,
    whipped
3 tbs brandy
icing sugar
50g/2 oz chocolate curls

Method
- Beat together the eggs and sugar until thick and peaky. Mix in the flour and chocolate powder.

- Pout into a Swiss roll tin lined with greaseproof paper.

- Cook for 15 minutes at 180C/350F/Gas 4.

- Turn cake out onto a wet teatowel with sugar sprinkled on it, and gently remove the greaseproof paper.

- Place a fresh piece of greaseproof paper on the cake and roll it up carefully, with paper between the layers. Leave to cool.

- To prepare the filling: drain the cherries, keeping 150ml/ a quarter pint of the juice.

- Pour the juice into a saucepan with the arrowroot and bring to the boil. Keep 8 cherries to one side and add the rest to the thickened syrup.

- Carefully unroll the cake and pour the brandy over it.

- Spread half the cream over the cake, followed by the cherry mixture.

- Carefully re-roll the cake and decorate with the cream, chocolate curls and cherries.

RASPBERRY *MERINGUE* CAKE

One of my favourite fruits is raspberry, and in the summer, raspberry and meringue are the perfect combination.

Ingredients
The Meringue
4 egg whites
225g/8 oz golden caster sugar
115g/4 oz walnuts, finely chopped

The Filling
275ml/ half a pint of double cream
lemon rind
450g/1 lb raspberries
1 tbs lemon curd

Method
- Whisk the egg whites until firm.

- Gradually add the sugar, beating until peaky and glossy, then add the walnuts.

- Grease and line two 8" (21cm) cake tins and divide the mixture between them. Bake the *meringue* for 90 minutes at 160C/ 325F/Gas 3.

- When ready, cool on a wire rack.

- To prepare the filling: beat the cream, add the lemon curd and lemon rind. Spread the mixture onto one *meringue* and place the other *meringue* on top.

- Keep aside some raspberries for decoration and whizz the rest in a food processor for 1-2 minutes. Sieve to remove the seeds and pour the juice around the *meringue*.

- Dust icing sugar over the whole thing and decorate with raspberries.

APRICOT CHOCOLATE PUDDING

The idea for this pudding came to me one Sunday, when my daughter-in-law phoned to say she was coming to lunch with two friends from Barnsley, and four children between them! I hunted in my kitchen cupboards for possible pudding ingredients. Well, all I had was a tin of apricot pie filling and a tasty chunk of chocolate, so on my marks, and off I went!

Ingredients

175g/6 oz softened butter
175g/6 oz caster sugar
3 eggs
175g/6 oz self-raising flour
1 tsp baking powder

50g/2 oz ground almonds
25g/1 oz cocoa
a few drops vanilla essence
1 400g/14 oz tin apricot pie filling

Method

- In a large bowl, cream the butter, sugar and eggs until light and fluffy.

- Add the sieved flour, baking powder and cocoa, with the almonds and vanilla essence, using a metal spoon to keep the mixture light.

- Grease an 8" (21 cm) ovenproof dish or a 2 pint (1.2l) tin. Put half the mixture in the bottom, spread the pie filling over it and the remaining cake over the filling.

- Bake for 40 minutes at 180C/350F/Gas 4.

TIP: Serve with a delicious chocolate sauce: 225g/8 oz good quality chocolate, and 570ml/1 pint double cream. Heat slowly in a saucepan until the chocolate has melted and blended with the cream.

FILO STRAWBERRY TART

A delicious, light summer tart, very easy to make for those who can't make pastry.

Ingredients
6 leaves filo pastry
50g/2 oz butter
450g/1 lb lemon curd
275ml/ half a pint of double cream
1 packet strawberry jelly
450g/1 lb strawberries

a 9" (23 cm) ovenproof plate

Method
● Grease the plate well with butter. Place filo leaves on the plate and brush with remaining butter. Line the filo with foil filled with baking beans. Bake blind for 10 minutes at 190C/375F/ Gas 5 until the filo is golden and crisp.

● Remove the foil and baking beans.

● Melt the jelly with 275ml/ half a pint of boiling water, and leave to half-set.

● Spread the lemon curd over the pastry. Beat the cream until thick, then spread over the lemon curd.

● Arrange sliced strawberries on top of the tart, keeping some for decoration.

● Pour the jelly over the strawberries and leave to set through. Decorate with remaining strawberries.

CHILDREN'S CHRISTMAS CHOCOLATE PUDDING

Children of all ages will love this wickedly yummy pudding.

Ingredients
450g/1 lb milk chocolate
425ml/ three quarters of a pint of double cream
115g/4 oz colourful cherries, finely chopped
115g/4 oz walnuts, finely chopped
50g/2 oz currants
50g/2 oz sultanas
50g/2 oz raisins
50g/2 oz ground almonds
225g/8 oz white chocolate

Method
- Whisk the cream until it thickens slightly.

- Melt the chocolate in a bowl over a pan of hot water.

- Add the dried ingredients and the melted chocolate to the cream and stir gently. Pour into a 900g/2 lb basin and freeze until required.

- On Christmas morning, remove the pudding from the freezer; it will thaw slightly by lunchtime. Melt the white chocolate in a bowl over hot water and pour over the pudding.

- Decorate with cherries and angelica or a sprig of holly.

TREACLE PUDDING

Ingredients
The Pudding
115g/4 oz sultanas, soaked in orange juice overnight
60ml/1 fl oz orange juice
115g/4 oz butter
50g/2 oz golden caster sugar
2 size 2 eggs
115g/4 oz golden syrup, warmed
175g/6 oz self-raising flour
115g/4 oz fresh brown breadcrumbs

a greased and lined 7-8" (18-21 cm) ovenproof dish or tin

The Syrup
225g/8 oz golden syrup
juice and rind 1 orange
1 tsp arrowroot

Method
- Cream the butter and sugar until light and fluffy. Beat in the eggs, one at a time, and beat in the warmed syrup.

- Fold in the flour, breadcrumbs, orange juice and sultanas. Pour into the dish/tin and cook for 50-60 minutes at 180C/350F/ Gas 4.

- To prepare the syrup: place all the ingredients in a saucepan and bring to the boil, stirring until it thickens.

- Serve the pudding with the syrup and *crème fraîche*.